dation

consolidation

CESAR CASTELLANOS D.

SEMINAR

LEVEL 3

TEACHERS' GUIDE

consol

CESAR CASTELLANOS D.© 2003
Published by G12 Editors
sales@g12bookstore.com

ISBN 1-932285-31-8

Made in Colombia

Printed in Colombia

CONTENTS

PREFACE

The material you now hold in your hands was birthed out of our own experience within the church through the leaders that we developed over the years, in ministry. Even though we knew from the day our church opened in 1983, that we would be a cell church and would have an immense effect on our city, it was not until sometime in 1990 that the Lord removed the veil to expose to us, the vision of the government of twelve. In the wake of this revelation, the church experienced a growth explosion that has superceded all records on church growth with no waning in sight. Along with the excitement of growth, as pastors we were challenged to develop these new believers that the Lord entrusted to us.

During this time God gave me a Rhema word for our ministry: "I will give you the ability to quickly train people." This was a word we truly needed because up until then, it was taking at least two years to train a cell leader. The demand was great and the process was just too long. But after that word, the heavens opened up and a special anointing was released upon each person that was helping us in the ministry. Now, the entire congregation, from the least to the greatest, reeled with motivation; they wanted to be a part of the vision. The mind of the people, even ours, was powerfully impressed with the vision of growth, but the necessary components were not in place for the most advantageous operating system.

A formula has been developed and implemented as a result of the word the Lord gave, thanks to the team of pastors and leaders that Jesus gave us. How would we actually train faster? What tools would be used? The best possible method was being created for our use according to the results we saw as we went along. We then decided to put them into motion as a part of our vision.

For many years prior, we did not want to be away from the church because we felt that our vision was still being established. Neither did we want to teach about church growth until we had a congregation to back it up. Now that God has allowed us to become one of the largest churches in the world, with an average of 25,000 leadership school students, we can only thank God for His mercy to our country and for having lifted up our church as the leader of that great spiritual awakening which has been able to influence the nations of the earth. It is our prayer that this material blesses your life, your church and your ministry. May each one of you fulfill God's purpose in your lives.

In the love of Christ,

Cesar and Claudia Castellanos.

Consolidation

TEACHING OBJECTIVE

The goal is that the students understand the purpose of consolidation.

STUDENT OBJECTIVE

1 Explain the purpose for the consolidation process.

2 Explain the work necessary for consolidation.

BIBLICAL FOUNDATIONAL
REFERENCE

Jhon 21:15 - 17

CORRESPONDING
BIBLICAL
FOUNDATION

Colossians 1:28-29

2 Timothy 1:1-11

1 Corinthians 3:6-9

Romans 1:9

PURPOSE

Today people are looking for answers for their spiritual and emotional needs. For this reason it is necessary to set up a standard by which the new believers can be cared for. As they begin to attend church, they will learn to seek the Lord and find out what purpose He has in store for them. This process of consolidation is the making of great leaders for Christ.

God's desire is that we develop a system of care for the new believers who He sees as little lambs and that we continue to follow up with them until they become sheep that are easily pastured.

Paul's example in " We proclaim him, admonishing and teaching everyone with all wisdom, so that we may present everyone perfect in Christ. To this end I labor, struggling with all his energy, which so powerfully works in me." (Colossians 1: 28, 29)

- Preach the gospel.
- Warn every man.
- Teach every man in all wisdom.
- To have the perfect plan of Christ is to care for every new believer.
- To allow God's power to fully flow through him in his work.

Paul the consolidator
2 Timothy 1:1-13

Paul opened his heart to his spiritual son, Timothy, whom he was consolidating and had fond memories of. Paul encourages him to:
V. 6. Stir up the gift of God which you have received.
V. 7. Not to give up God has not given us a spirit of fear but of self-control.
V. 8. To testify not being ashamed of our Lord.
V. 9. Be assured that he was called to (the) ministry.
V. 13. Hold fast to the sound doctrine you have received.
Guard the spiritual treasure received from the Holy Spirit.

We know that the calling of God for our lives is to take the Good News of salvation throughout the world. Along with that we must initiate the meticulous process of caring for the new believers by tending to them through continued contact so that they become strengthened and encouraged to become disciples of Christ. This is consolidation.

A. THE PURPOSE OF CONSOLIDATING A NEW CONVERT

- To show the benefits of belonging to the family of God.
- To show an interest in their needs.
- To offer fellowship.
- To water the seed that has been sown (1 Corinthians 3:6).
- To show them Christ, His love and His abundant life.
- To make them aware of their decision for Christ.
- To get them involved in the cell group activities.

B. THE WORK OF CONSOLIDATION

We need to understand that:

- We are God's fellow workers (1 Corinthians 3:9).
- Our calling is to produce (win) and retain fruit (John 15:5).
- We must make each new believer an effective leader (2 Timothy 2:2).

For this to occur it is necessary to:

- Pray for those that God has placed under our care (Romans 1:9).
- Spend time with them (Acts 19:8).
- Show an interest in their family (Acts 16:31-34).
- Feel a burden for their needs and problems (Acts 17:6).
- Have time for them when they need it (Acts 19:22-23).
- Whenever possible, meet their needs (Acts 11:29).

In Daniel's prayer (Daniel 9) for the restoration of his people, it shows us the steps that every consolidator needs to keep in mind:

- To have a profound compassion for the people.
- To stand in their place.
- To confess their sin as if it is your own.
- To beg for divine favor and mercy on their behalf.
- To fully trust in the quick restoration of their lives.

For consolidation to become more effective it is good to teach each cell member to adopt consolidation as a lifestyle.

CONCLUSION

Consolidation is vital to develop the vision and necessary to fulfill goals.

APPLICATION

During this trimester, purpose in your heart to take one new person each week to the cell group and put into practice the steps discussed in class.

EVALUATION

It will be necessary to find out the students' true understanding of what has been taught up to this point by giving a quiz or test.

RECOMMENDED METHODOLOGY

Lesson, part one – lecture.
Lesson, part two – hand out bible references. Have the student give interpretation (with teacher's help when needed).

STUDENTS' ASSIGNMENT

The student should search the bible for one example of consolidation and explain it.

1 Questionnaire for further study

1. What is consolidation?

_____

_____

_____

2. What is the main purpose of consolidation?

_____

_____

_____

3. How could I demonstrate the benefits of belonging to the family of God?

_____

_____

_____

4. How can I be an instrument of God to bring others to Christ?

_____

_____

5. What methods will help me to fulfill the calling of bringing people into the family of God and retaining them?

_____

_____

_____

6. Where is consolidation in the Ladder of Success?

_____

_____

7. Consider this:

How many people have you consolidated since you've been in Christ?

_____

_____

How many have remained?

_____

How many have left?

_____

How many do you continue caring for?

_____

Pray about your answers. If you need to ask the Lord for
forgiveness for what you have not done, then do so, make
restitution.

How to Consolidate

LESSON

TEACHING OBJECTIVE

The goal is that the students understand the basic principles needed to carry out effective consolidation.

STUDENT OBJECTIVE

Explain the best method of consolidation.

BIBLICAL FOUNDATIONAL REFERENCE

Acts 9:10-18

CORRESPONDING BIBLICAL FOUNDATION

John 3:16

Romans 3:12

Isaiah 53

Revelation 3:20

Acts 3:19

1 John 1:9

KEY VERSE

"The Lord told him, "Go to the house of Judas on Straight Street and ask for a man from Tarsus named Saul, for he is praying"
(Acts 9:11)

HOW TO CONSOLIDATE

It is recommended that the same person, who evangelized the new believer, to also do the consolidation because of the pre-established friendship and trust. It is important that each member in the cell group knows how to consolidate. If you are a cell leader, you must take the time to show them understanding that the teaching requires uninterrupted time.

You should follow these steps:

1. Explain the plan of salvation by using these 5 teachings:

a. Love (John 3:16 and John 10:10b).
b. Sin (Roman 3:12 and 23).
c. Jesus the only and sufficient Savior (John 14:6, Galatians 3:13, Ephesians 2:8-9 and Isaiah 53).
d. Repentance (Acts 3:19, 1 John 1:9, Isaiah 1:18 and Proverbs 28:13).
e. Accepting and Receiving (Revelations 3:20 and John 1:12).

2. Get to know how to resolve their doubts or questions that they are having regarding the Bible, the church and God

Answer the people's questions about:

- Faith
- The after-life
- Finances
- Family

3. Identify their needs and problems as you show interest in them

- Teach them to ask God in faith and give them your prayer support.
- Provide them with biblical passages that will strengthen them and show them God's point of view.
- Be motivating and wise in counsel so that they can be the decision makers.
- If you can, help them financially.
- Get them involved within your ministry's activities.

4. Have success during the process

- Understand that new believers have doubts and questions that should be resolved.
- Not all people respond the same way. Some take more time than others do.
- Gain the confidence of their family without having attitudes that may be taken as abrasive. Guard your image and the church's.
- Show respect for everything (work, investments, family, etc.). Later, you will have the opportunity to instruct the person in making godly decisions.
- Show them how important they are as people, not just as numbers to reach a goal.
- Motivate them in faith constantly.
- Do not pressure them. Be flexible.
- Involve them in activities and make them feel important.
- Never make coming to church seem like switching religions.
- Introduce people to them with whom they can establish friendships.

CONCLUSION

The ability to accomplish an excellent consolidation is acquired as we prepare ourselves and do it constantly.

APPLICATION

Develop a workshop for your disciples that will them the criteria needed to make effective consolidations.

EVALUATION

Use an exam or quiz to find out the students' true understanding of what has been taught in class.

RECOMMENDED METHODOLOGY

Use visual aids to enhance the lecture and allow the students to share experiences about their personal consolidation experience.

STUDENTS' ASSIGNMENT

The students should bring to class information about their consolidation process of one or two people they have won in the past week.

2 Questionnaire for further study

1. What should I do to accomplish an excellent consolidation?

_____

_____

_____

2. How would you share the plan of salvation with someone?

_____

_____

_____

3. What are the 5 basic teachings about sharing Christ?

_____

_____

_____

_____

4. Match by drawing a line from the teachings to their matching verses.

The teaching on love
The teaching on sin
The teaching on Christ as the only and sufficient savior
The teaching on repentance
The teaching on accepting/ receiving Christ

(John 3:16, John 10:10b and Romans 3:12 and 23)
(John 14:6, Galatians 3:13, Ephesians 2:8-9 and Isaiah 53)
(Acts 3:19, 1John1: 9, Isaiah 1:18 and Proverbs 28:13)
(Revelations 3:20 and John 1:12)

5. How would you respond if someone asked these questions?

a. Do you believe in the Virgin Mary? _____

_____

_____

_____

b. What is the difference between Catholics and Protestants?

_____

_____

_____

c. Are you talking about another religion?

_____

_____

_____

d. What are tithes and offerings for?

_____

_____

_____

e. What does the Pastor do?

_____

_____

_____

_____

6. What should I do after I testify to someone?

a. _____

b. _____

c. _____

d. _____

e. _____

f. _____

g. _____

7. What should I do while in the process of consolidation?

_____

_____

_____

_____

The Fruit of the Holy Spirit

LESSON

TEACHING OBJECTIVE

The goal is that the student understands the importance of knowing the Holy Spirit and to long for Him with all of their heart.

STUDENT OBJECTIVE

1 Explain what fruit means.

2 Identify which areas in your life are related to the fruit of the Spirit.

BIBLICAL FOUNDATIONAL REFERENCE

Galatians 5:22-23

CORRESPONDING BIBLICAL FOUNDATION

Proverbs 8:19 , 10:16

KEY VERSE

"But the fruit of the
Spirit is love, joy,
peace, patience,
kindness, goodness,
faithfulness, gentleness
and self-control"
(Galatians 5:22-23)

PURPOSE

To be able to establish the fruit of the Holy Spirit as a manifestation of the character of God in our lives. Our attitudes should exemplify His character.

The Fruit of the Spirit

The gifts represent the capacity or the power in the believer. The fruit represents the character. Both compliment each other.

The fruit of the Holy Spirit is love, joy, peace, patience, kindness, goodness, faithfulness, gentleness and self-control. Against such things there is no law (Galatians 5:22-23).

LOVE

A new command I give to you, that you love one another. As I have loved you, so you must love one another. By this all will know that you are my disciples, if you have love for one another (John 13:34-35). The fulfillment of the law is love (Romans 13:9-10).

Now the purpose of the commandment is love from a pure heart, from a good conscience and from sincere faith, from which some, having strayed, have turned aside to idle talk (1Timothy 1:5-6).

When referring to love, the Greek language uses several different words some of the ones found in the New Testament are:

Filia/ Phileo (love between friends), Agape (pure and enduring love, which is the love that was manifested and created by God). There are other greek words for love that are not found in the New Testament.

Agape love comes forth from the believer when the Word of God has been deposited in the heart and has taken the believer to a new birth (John 15:12-13).

JOY

The New Illustrated Bible Dictionary says: "Joy is what man desires and what he seeks. He finds it when he finds God. Only then will he retain it, according to his growth in the knowledge of God" (page 435). This means that God is the only source of joy. This "fruit" grows as your direct, personal relationship with God continues.

True joy is found when a repented man turns his eyes and heart to God. Then the Holy Spirit allows that person to recognize what it means to live in the kingdom of God because "the kingdom of God is not food or drink but righteousness, peace and joy in the Holy Spirit" (Romans 14:17).

Joy is what allows every believer to stay strong in the midst of the pressure brought on by circumstances (Habakkuk 3:17-18).

PEACE

In a general sense, peace can be defined as absence of conflict. But true peace is that which is obtained and after reconciled. For example, when there has been a situation of conflict among two people or nations or sides, only when there is a dialogue that leads them to, make a pact or to reconcile could we say that everything has returned to normal and peace has been obtained.

Colossians 1:19-20: Through Him all things were reconciled.

Romans 5:1: Therefore, having been justified by faith, we have peace with God through our Lord Jesus Christ.

Ephesians 2:14-15: He has made both one and has broken down the wall of separation.

Isaiah 9:7: Of the increase of His government and peace there will be no end.

Isaiah 48:18: Oh, that you had heeded my commandments! Then your peace would be like a river and your righteousness like the waves of the sea.

PATIENCE

Patience is considered a virtue. Within its definition is the command to voluntarily suffer through adversity while waiting for something. This implies that the believer endures trials without murmuring or complaining.

Romans 5:3-4: We glory in the tribulations knowing that tribulation produces patience.

The development of patience is that human virtue emanating from God, through the Holy Spirit. It contributes to the strengthening of character. To fulfill this objective, it is important for everyone to have two goals in common: To be firm in enduring problems and slow to take vengeance against harm received.

Isaiah 53:3-7: He was oppressed and He was afflicted, yet He opened not His mouth.

1 Peter 2:20-23: But when you do good and suffer, if you take it patiently, this is commendable before God.

KINDNESS

Kindness is associated with benevolence, compassion, mercy and godliness. This fruit of the Spirit consists of treating others as we would like to be treated by them.

More than a suggestion, kindness is a mandate from Jesus to His disciples and to us.

Luke 6:27-31 From this passage we learn various manifesta-

tions of the fruit of kindness:
1. Love our enemies.
2. Do good to those who despise us.
3. Bless those who curse us.
4. Pray for those who slander.
5. Be willing to be tolerant (offer the other cheek).
6. Give to them what they want to take from us.

GOODNESS

Although there is a relationship between goodness and kindness, the first makes reference to the way in which we should live because it gives testimony of the existence of God. Derek Prince says, "The goodness of God in the life of a believer confronts the world with God's existence."

The biblical concept of goodness includes [moral] excellence. It applies primarily to God because according to what Jesus says, He is the only one that is good.

In Mark 10:17-18 Jesus said to the rich young ruler, "Why do you call me 'good'? No one is good but One, that is, God." In other words, goodness is based on what God is and does because He is the only one in whom we find moral excellence, together with perfection; due to His integrity and righteousness.

FAITH

Those who possess the gift of faith can easily move in the supernatural dimension. They may call that which is not as if it were. They can unleash life where there is death and healing where there is sickness. They can bring prosperity where there is scarcity. It is the means by which God uses to bring revival to churches, cities and nations.

Hebrews 11

Vs. 1. Conceive a miracle in the heart and speak about it as if it had already taken place.
Vs. 2 For by faith the elders passed their tests.
Vs. 3 It brings renewal of the mind so the Word of God can be revealed.

Vs. 4 It moves us to give our best to God.

Vs. 5 Without faith it is impossible to please God.

Vs. 6 God rewards those who diligently seek Him.

Vs. 7 It prepares it an atmosphere for the salvation of your family.

Vs. 8 Learn to hear God and obey Him.

Vs. 9 -10 We are sure that our true citizenship is in His glory.

Vs. 11 It makes us fathers of a multitude.

Vs. 20 We can bless our children and our disciples.

MEEKNESS

Meekness allows us to have enough will power, (given by the Father) not to let our circumstances overcome us and affect our enthusiasm. Meekness is a special grace given to Christians by the Holy Spirit.

It demonstrates the authority in all those who possess it.

Proverbs 16:32 He who is slow to anger is better than a warrior, who takes a city.

2 Timothy 1:7 For God has not given us a spirit of fear but of power and of love and of a sound mind.

Numbers 12:3 Now, Moses was very humble, (meek) more than all men who were on the face of the earth. To reach this level of maturity he had to be broken in the desert.

Psalm 51:17 The sacrifices of God are a broken spirit; a broken and contrite heart. These, oh, God, you will not despise.

Matthew 5:5 Blessed are the meek for they will inherit the earth.

SELF-CONTROL

Self-control is a manifestation of the Holy Spirit defined by the capacity to improve any weakness.

Self-control is related to prudence and is distinct in the believer who is guided by the Holy Spirit. It shows itself in wise behavior.

Philippians 2:12b-13 ...work out your own salvation with fear and trembling, for it is God who works in you both to will and to do for His good pleasure.

Self-control originates in God and He expects us to manifest it by showing sobriety which depends on our will.

1 Corinthians 9:25 And everyone who competes for the prize is temperate in all things.

James 1:12 ...the crown of life which the Lord has promised to those who love Him.

Philippians 3:14 I press toward the goal for the prize of the upward call of God in Christ Jesus.

EVALUATION

The student should make a comparative graph of the fruit of the Holy Spirit and the opposite characteristics. They should follow this with an examination of their own character and write down those things that they should personally renounce.

RECOMMENDED METHODOLOGY

A good way to initially explain what each characteristic of the Fruit of the Spirit consists of is to ask the students to explain what the opposite characteristics are.

STUDENTS' ASSIGNMENT

Have the students find out what fruits of the Holy Spirit they have and which ones they still lack.

3 Questionnaire for further study

1. Who is the Holy Spirit?

_____
_____
_____
_____

2. What is the Holy Spirit's ministry?

_____
_____
_____
_____

3. Are you conscious of the work of the Holy Spirit in your life?

_____
_____
_____
_____

4. What has the Holy Spirit done in your life?

_____
_____
_____
_____

5. Define the word Fruit.

_____
_____
_____

6. What is the fruit of the Spirit?

_____
_____
_____
_____

The Gifts of the Holy Spirit

4

TEACHING OBJECTIVE

That the students understand which are the gifts of the Holy Spirit and how essential they are in carrying out the ministry.

STUDENT OBJECTIVE

1 Define what gifts are and what attitude we should have toward them.

2 Explain each one of the gifts and their relationship to the calling of God.

3 Explain each one of the ministerial gifts.

BIBLICAL FOUNDATIONAL
REFERENCE

1 Corinthians 12:4-11

CORRESPONDING
BIBLICAL
FOUNDATION

1 Corinthians 12:7-10

Exodus 18:14-27

Acts 6:4

Ecclesiastes 10:10

Proverbs 2:6

GIFTS OF THE SPIRIT

Is also known as charisma, a word that comes from the original Greek charis meaning grace, favor, power, office and mission.

The gifts have been given by God to be administered in the church to the glory of the name of Jesus. 1 Corinthians 12:7-10.

The gifts are classified in the following groups:
A. Revelation: A word of wisdom, word of knowledge and discernment of spirits.
B. Power: Faith, healing and miracles.
C. Inspiration (verbal): Prophesy, tongues and interpretation of tongues.

GIFTS OF REVELATION

Word of wisdom

In Exodus 18:14-27 God gives Moses a word of wisdom through his father-in-law.

The apostles taught the same thing and chose deacons to help them so that they could focus on the most important part of their ministry: Prayer, Studying and the Preaching of the Word (Acts 6:4).

"If the ax is dull and its edge unsharpened, more strength is needed but skill will bring success" (Ecclesiastes 10:10).

Wisdom directs. It lets you know the most effective way to complete a task; having our weapons ready at all times says we are wise. The work of the preacher is more efficient when his biblical knowledge is sharpened and his prayer life is specific and on-going.

It means working under the complete direction of the Holy Spirit to avoid fatigue. "For the Lord (Jehovah) gives wisdom and from His mouth comes knowledge and intelligence" (Proverbs 2:6). "But the wisdom from above is first pure, then peaceable, gentle, reasonable, full of mercy and good fruits" (James 3:17).

Word of Knowledge

The word of wisdom is directional while the word of knowledge is informative.

The prophet Elisha knew each move of the King of Aram and for this reason he was able to inform the King of Israel, preventing the ambush that had been prepared for them (2 Kings 6:8-13).

Acts 5:1-10. Peter was able to discern the way Satan had filled the hearts of Ananias and Sapphira of tempting them and to lie to the Holy Spirit. This could have stalled the growth of the church if it had not been detected, for it had contaminated many, as with the sins of Achan, who lied, stole and deceived. For the same reason, Israel was defeated in battle by the insignificant army of Ai (Joshua 7:11-12).

Read Acts 5:12 and discover that because of the word of knowledge brought to Peter by the Holy Spirit the Lord backed all of His apostles with signs and wonders.

By the word of knowledge, God kept the church from divisions and has maintained all the leadership in unity and harmony. This gift is like a lighthouse that keeps our lives, homes and ministries from harm.

Discernment of spirits

In the end times the forces of darkness will work like never be-fore to destroy the greatest number of people ever. One of the schemes that the enemy uses is deception. It is intended to separate the believer from the truth. For this reason the love of many will grow cold. Therefore, it is imperative that the gift of the discernment of spirits be revived in the hearts of the leaders so that they are able to keep the purity of the truth and evade any other doctrine of error. (Ephesians 6:10-13)

> Demons know those who
> can defeat them
> Mark 1:24

Being the light of this world, wherever Jesus went, He would uncover the works of darkness and the unveiled demon was overcome. When the gift of discernment of spirits operates inside the church, we will easily move according to divine direction. If a demonic power needs to be broken, we do it. If it requires a miracle, we ask God so that it would occur; keeping in mind that God is always leading us.

Fear, religiosity, oppression, infirmity and divination are some of the spirits that should be discerned inside the church so that later we can begin the process of deliverance for the affected persons.

The gift of discernment of spirits, is most critical during the encounters. It helps make the ministering more effective (Acts 16:17-18).

GIFTS OF POWER

The gift of faith

The Gifts-of-Power group is headed by the gift of faith followed by healings and miracles. These three manifestations of the Holy Spirit are interwoven and have perfect harmony among the three. Faith is required in every area of our Christian life. The great enemy of faith is doubt and it is accompanied by fear. God has allowed us all to have access to Him through faith in Jesus Christ. "...without faith it is impossible to please God" (Hebrews 11:6).

We need faith to relate intimately with the All-powerful (James 2:23).

Jesus said, "Have faith, the faith of God" (Mark 11:22-24).

The gift of faith takes us outside of a natural state and into a supernatural way of life that gives our spiritual eyes the capacity to clearly perceive the invisible. At the same time, the Word of God takes on the true worth for our lives. It produces a supernatural strength to challenge and conquer even the impossible. It assures us that the Lord will give us the victory. This gift kept three Hebrew young men from dying by fire. (Daniel 3:28-29) Romans 8:11 is a portion of scripture that gave me, Cesar Castellanos life when I was dying.

By faith, Jesus spoke and the fig tree dried up (Mark 11:14).
The Lord will back everything we say. (Mark 11:22-23).
The Lord does not ask for a mountain of faith, only enough faith to move mountains (Luke 17:6-7).

Gifts of Healing(s)

This gift is mentioned in a plural tense because it leads us to believe that it can be manifested in every type of disease.

David said that God was interested in healing all of our infirmities (Psalm 103:1-4).

We know that through sin, the curse of sickness came into mankind.

- The mission of evil (such as sickness) is to kill, steal and destroy (John 10:10).
- Jesus came to undo the works of the devil (1 John 3:8).
- Jesus had the anointing to heal the sick (Isaiah 61:1-2).
- Peter said that Jesus had the anointing to heal all those who were oppressed by the devil because God was with Him (Acts 10:38).
- Isaiah prophetically revealed the victory of the cross (Isaiah 53:4-5).

Only when the redemptive work of Jesus on the cross is

understood, can the gifts of healing operate within an individual. When that veil is removed and the understanding has come into the heart and mind, then everyone can visualize clearly all the miracles that have already been conquered by the Lord on the cross.

- Jesus healed all the sick (Luke 4:40).
- Jesus gave this same authority to His twelve (Matthew 10:1).
- Jesus said these signs will follow those that believe (Mark 16:17-18).

The Lord has always used healing to bless people and likewise has the door open so that all can receive the message of salvation.

Gift of Miracles

There is a narrow relationship between the gift of healings and the gift of miracles. Sometimes in can be difficult to know the difference.

A miracle is a supernatural act that has occurred without human intervention.

Moses was one of the men of old, most used by God for miracles: The ten plagues of Egypt, the parting of the Red Sea, the miracle of the bitter waters, manna raining from heaven for forty years, the water flowing from the rock, the quails, etc. None of these things have any other explanation except divine intervention. Exodus 15:26 says if they obeyed the word, God would heal them.

- Joshua made the sun and the moon stop from moving in the battle against Gideon and there has never been another day like that one (Joshua 10:12-14).
- God caused time to go back by 40 minutes (10 degrees), in response to Ezekiel.
- Jesus changed the water into wine at the wedding of Cana (John 2:1-12).
- He created eyes for the blind man just by putting mud in his eye sockets (John 9:1-12).
- The wind and the sea obeyed the word of authority that came from the lips of Jesus.

Among the gifts of inspiration are: The gift of prophecy, The gift of tongues, The gift of interpretation of tongues; which the Lord has permitted to be used by the spoken word.

Gift of Prophecy

Jesus came as the fulfillment of the prophetic word (Hebrews 1:1-3)

In 2 Peter 1:16-21 the apostle points out:

- The prophetic word is sure.
- We should pay attention to it.
- It is a lamp in the darkness.
- It is not for private interpretation.
- It does not come through human will.
- Prophets were inspired by the Spirit of God.

In 1 Corinthians 14:3, Paul taught that prophecy was for edification, exhortation and comfort.

1 Corinthians 14:1 declares that it should be one of the most desirable gifts.

1 Thessalonians 5:19-22 Do not quench the Spirit; do not despise prophetic utterances. But examine everything carefully; hold fast to that which is good; abstain from every form of evil.

Gift of Tongues

The manifestation of the Holy Spirit is evidenced through the gift of tongues which is defined as the ability to speak in other languages that the person speaking has not previously learned.

Acts 2:1-13: On the day of Pentecost, the 120 were filled with the Holy Spirit and spoke in other tongues. They were together in one accord when suddenly there came from heaven a noise like a violent rushing wind, and it filled the whole house where they were sitting.

Luke 24:49: God promised they would be vested with power from on high.

Acts 1:8: "But you shall receive power." The purpose of tongues is:

- To have intimate fellowship with God 1 Corinthians 14:2
- For personal edification 1 Corinthians 14:4
- To edify the whole church 1 Corinthians 14:5
- To minister to the unbelievers   1 Corinthians 14:22

Paul dedicated most of his time to praying in tongues. "I thank God that I speak in tongues more than all of you" (1 Corinthians 14:18).

Gift of interpretation of tongues

The gift of tongues together with the gift of interpretation of tongues equals prophecy.

1 Corinthians 14: 27-28 explains it like this: If anyone speaks in an unknown tongue, it should be by two or at most three, each taking his turn and one must interpret.

Paul tried to bring clarity and prevent disorder in the church by providing an explanation; he said that just as the gift of tongues was given to the church, the Holy Spirit is manifested through the gift of interpretation of tongues.

The possibility of interpretation of tongues enriches the gifts of the Spirit by opening the opportunity for the whole church to be blessed by them. Both of these gifts, speaking in tongues and interpretation of tongues are basically intertwined and when anointed, a prophetic manifestation comes forth. The interpretation under the anointing of the Holy Spirit is for the congregation to understand the language being spoken by the person that God has chosen.

·   1 Corinthians 14:5 it is for the edification of the church.

·   1 Corinthians 14:13 you should pray for the interpretation.

WHAT OUR ATTITUDE SHOULD BE TOWARDS THE GIFTS OF THE SPIRIT

1. Do not be ignorant 1 Corinthians 12:1
2. Do not be careless 1 Timothy 4:14
3. Desire them and seek them 1 Corinthians 12:31 and 14:12
4. Revive them 2 Timothy 1:6
5. The highest motivation for exercising the spiritual gifts is love
   1 Corinthians 13:1 and 12:7 and 31

CONCLUSION

To receive the gifts, the fruit of the spirit needs to control our lives. The Holy Spirit is the essence of our ministry because it equips us to function with power.

EVALUATION

When you test the students, notice the explanations they use and ask them to express themselves about the overall lesson. Have them clearly explain the difference between the Fruit of the Spirit and the Gifts of the Spirit.

RECOMMENDED METHODOLOGY

For the Gifts of the Spirit, the teacher should prepare hand-outs that explain each one. After a time of research, using their study bibles, allow the students to make presentations to the rest of the class using skits or dramatizations to show how the gifts work. The teacher should be willing to guide this activity, clearing up any doubts and pointing out key facts. This class can also be taught by a lecture.

STUDENTS' ASSIGNMENT

The students should examine their own lives to see what gifts are functioning and which ones are not and why.

4 Questionnaire for Further Study

1. What does the word gift mean?

_____

_____

_____

2. List the gifts of the Spirit:

_____

_____

_____

3. How are the gifts divided into groups?

    a._____

    b._____

    c._____

4. What are the gifts for?

_____

_____

_____

_____

5. What should our attitude be towards the gifts?

_____

_____

6. Explain each of the gifts of the Spirit:

_____

_____

_____

_____

_____

_____

_____

_____

_____

_____

_____
_____
_____
_____

7. Who is the giver of the gifts?

_____
_____
_____
_____

8. How can I get the gifts of the Holy Spirit?

_____
_____
_____
_____

Ministry Gifts

5
LESSON

TEACHING OBJECTIVE

The student should understand the function and inter-relationships of each of the ministerial gifts.

STUDENT OBJECTIVE

1   Explain the general function of the ministry gifts.

2   Explain the function of each of the ministries.

3   Explain the relationship between the ministries.

BIBLICAL FOUNDATIONAL REFERENCE

Ephesians 4:11

CORRESPONDING BIBLICAL FOUNDATION

Acts 26:19

1 Corinthians 9:2

Hebrews 2:4

John 17

Acts 4:33

Acts 5:12

Acts 8:18

PURPOSE

To clearly establish the significance of each of the ministry gifts and know their relationships that exist among them.

THE APOSTOLIC MINISTRY

Ephesians 4:11 And
He gave some as apostles...

After spending all night in prayer, Jesus chose twelve
men to train and to continue the ministry He had
begun. He called them apostles and they were with
the Lord the entire time and it was very clear that
they kept the number twelve in that apostleship.
When Judas was no longer with them, they prayed and
chose his successor.

Marvin Vincent notes three qualities of an apostle:

a. He has had a visible encounter with the resurrected
   Christ.
b. He plants or starts churches.
c. His ministry is marked by signs, wonders and
   miracles.

In general, people who have had a supernatural
experience, where the Lord has revealed Himself to
them in a special way, whether in the beginning when
they first converted or later on during their ministry
training, have had a greater sensibility for being in this
type of ministry.

The greatest example is the apostle Paul. After Jesus
had already ascended to heaven, he revealed himself
to Paul as he was traveling on the road to Damascus.

From that day on, the Lord called him. In his testimony before King Agrippa, he said, "I did not prove to be disobedient to the heavenly vision" Acts 26:19. None of the other apostles worked as hard as Paul did to establish Christianity in different places. In his letter to the Corinthians he said, "If to others I am not an apostle, at least I am to you; for you are the seal of my apostleship in the Lord." (1 Corinthians 9:2). He exercised his apostleship by establishing a firm foundation in the lives of the people so that later they could reproduce themselves in others. This caused the work of God to last. Paul was a leader with results, setting a precedent in the ministry. Leaders who work in the ministry should show concrete results. Wherever he ministered, signs and wonders followed him. With just fragments of his clothing, people were healed and demons were cast out of their bodies.

In the intercessory prayer written in John 17, Jesus said:

Vs. 6
The twelve belonged to the Father and He gave them to Jesus.
Vs. 8
Jesus revealed Himself to them because of their faith.
Vs. 14
They received His Word and this made them different.
Vs. 18
In the same way Jesus was sent, they were also sent.
Acts 4:33
They testified with great power.
Acts 5:12
God worked supernaturally through the hands of the apostles.
Acts 8:18
The people received the Spirit when the apostles laid hands on them.
1 Timothy 2:4, 7
Paul's apostleship was the salvation of all men.
2 Timothy 1:11
Paul knew God had established him as a preacher, apostle and teacher.
Hebrews 3:1
We should study in detail how the Lord fulfilled His apostleship.

Ephesians 4:11 ...and some as prophets

The character of Christ is reflected in the five fold ministries. In the prophetic ministry, Jesus takes the mouth of the prophet and makes it His. In general, the prophet reveals future events. Prophet comes from a Greek word meaning forward and to speak. Moses was one of the greatest prophets that Israel had. Whenever Moses spoke, he shook the spiritual realm. His word was powerful enough to break the pride of Egypt and to deliver the Israelites from captivity. God promised Moses that He would raise up another prophet like himself, putting His words in his mouth and whoever did not obey would have to give an account to God (Acts 3:22). Jesus was recognized as the prophet that God spoke about. He established some as apostles and some as prophets. It pleased God to continue revealing His will through His prophets.

Acts 10:43   The main message is that if everyone believes in Jesus, they will receive forgiveness.

Acts 13:1   The early church was characterized by having prophets.

James 5:10   The apostle invites us to persevere by the example of the prophets.

2 Peter 1:19-21 The most important prophecy of all is the Bible because the Spirit of God inspired the prophets.

Acts 14:3   The prophet's message should be for edification, exhortation and comfort.

It is important not to impart fear to your disciples. They should be following Jesus out of love and not fear. The message of condemnation has done a lot of damage in the church of Jesus Christ. Most people live under extreme pressure due to their thoughts, jobs, homes and friends. This makes them feel condemned. What they want to find most, when they start going to a Christian church, is an ointment, to free them from all of their burdens. That's why, as spokespersons of Jesus, we should give them words of hope, motivation and comfort to create in them a desire to go on.

Ephesians 4:11 ...and some as evangelists

Evangelist comes from the Greek language also. It means to announce the good news of salvation. One of the characteristics of an evangelist is the grace of God that is upon him to draw people to God by hearing the message of salvation.

They have a word that is able to destroy the structures that non-believers have built up in their minds. The greatest evangelists are those who are in love with Jesus. We call it abiding in their first love (Revelation 2: 4-5). The Samaritan woman went and preached the good news to her city on the very day that she had her personal encounter with Jesus. As a result, many in the city of Samaria came to Christ (John 4:39). The main focus of the evangelist is to reach the unbelievers with the message of hope and salvation of the gospel.

Isaiah 53:1 Who has believed our report? And to whom is the arm of the Lord revealed?

The first question shows us three parts:

- The one announcing the gospel.
- The one receiving the message.
- The one believing the message.

The second question of the prophet is as a result of the first one. To those who believe, God will reveal Himself with all the benefits of the cross. The arm of the Lord implies the saving, healing, delivering and restoring power of God.

When Phillip, the evangelist, comes close to the eunuch, he is surprised to find him reading Isaiah 53. Phillip takes advantage of this—to preach the gospel of Jesus Christ. As a result, this man believed and was baptized and continued on his way with joy. (Acts 8:26-39)

Paul also knew of the great responsibility of preaching the gospel because God had given him that mission. That's why he said, "Woe unto me if I don't preach the gospel." (1 Corinthians 9:16). God opened the apostle's spiritual eyes for him to see the devastating effects that would come upon him if he failed to preach the gospel. How many souls would perish because of this? Paul accepted this great challenge and became all of those things, to all men, to win them to Christ (1Corinthians 9:22). In his farewell speech to the believers in Miletus he said, "For I did not shrink from declaring to you the whole purpose of God" (Acts 20:27).

Everyone, who has had a personal encounter with Jesus Christ, receives the benefit of, that which, Jesus paid for his or her sins. But he then takes on another task to help mankind pay off their debts through Jesus Christ. (Romans 1:14-15) Paul knew that the debt he owed the world was to take them the message of salvation and to not be ashamed of doing so because:

- It is the power of God unto salvation for those who believe.
- The righteousness of God is revealed by faith.
- Faith is the life giving righteousness of God (Rom. 1:16,17).

THE PASTORAL MINISTRY

Ephesians 4:11 ...and some as pastors

Pastor = shepherd of sheep: The one who cares for, guides, gives affection to and protects.

The pastoral ministry is very close to the divine character since God has revealed himself as the shepherd of his people. He shepherded Israel for forty years in the wilderness.

David, from a young age, shepherded his father's sheep and got to know the different aspects of being a pastor. He said in Psalm 23:

Vs. 1 The Lord is my shepherd; I shall not want (permanent provision).

Vs. 2 He leads his flock into satisfaction and prosperity.

Vs. 3 He knows how to correctly motivate and guide his sheep.

Vs. 4 He is with his flock even in difficult times, guiding and protecting.

Vs. 5 He prepares his messages carefully for his flock to enjoy a spiritual banquet.

Vs.6 He can pastor correctly and with mercy.

The Lord told the people of Israel that if they converted, He would give them shepherds after His own heart. (Jeremiah 3:14-15) They would feed them, give them security and they would multiply (Jeremiah 23:3-4).
Through Ezekiel the prophet, the Lord shows us how to pastor correctly:

Ezekiel 34:

Vs.3   Feed the flock.
Vs.4   Strengthen the sickly, heal the diseased, bind up the broken, do not lord over them and do not be harsh or violent towards them.
Vs.5   Guide them down the right path, protect them from the beasts and keep the flock together.
Vs.6   He has the anointing to rescue the ones who are lost. He searches diligently for them and inquires of their well being.
Vs.7   He knows he must answer to the Lord for every one of those sheep God has put in his hands.
Vs.10 They should have a heart like David.
Vs.24 He should guide the sheep into a solid relationship with God.
Vs.25 And God will make a covenant with them and protect them and give them security.
Vs.26 God will bless them and all that surrounds them.
Vs.27 He will prosper them and deliver them from oppression.
Vs.28 They will live with security.
Vs.29 He will honor them and give them abundance.
Vs.30 And they will know the Lord is with them.
Vs.31 Sheep are people.

In John 10 Jesus said:

Vs.7   He is the door of the sheep.
Vs.9   Whoever receives him will be saved.
Vs.10 He came to give us life and life in abundance.
Vs.11 He gives his life for his sheep.
Vs.14 He knows his sheep.
Vs.16 He does not discriminate.

Vs.28 He gives eternal life.

According to Hebrews 13:17, believers should obey their pastors and submit to them.

Paul encouraged his disciple in 2 Timothy 2:15-25 to:

Vs.15 Be diligent presenting yourself approved by God; as a workman who does not need to be ashamed, accurately handling the word of truth.
Vs.16 Avoid empty chatter.
Vs.21 Be purified to be used by God.
Vs.22 Flee from youthful lusts.
Vs.23 Refuse foolish discussions.
Vs.24 Be kind, teachable and patient when wronged.
Vs.25 Correct with gentleness.

2 Timothy 3:14 Persevere in the teachings you have received.
2 Timothy 4:2 Always be ready to preach the word with motivation, patience and doctrine.
2 Timothy 4:3-4 Keep people from myths.

THE TEACHING MINISTRY

Ephesians 4:11 ...and he set some as teachers

This is another one of the gifts that represent an extension of the character of Christ. Jesus told his disciples: You call me teacher and rightly so because I am. (John 13:13) One of the warnings that He gave his disciples was that they not wear the title, Rabbi; "...for One is your Teacher." (Matt 23:8) Even the religious leaders recognized Jesus as the one who had come from God, as a teacher because of the signs that followed Him. (John 3:2)

In Hebrews 5:12 the writer exhorts them saying that somewhere along their path of life they took a detour and because of this, they have to start over again with the spiritual milk of the word. James speaks of the responsibility of a teacher in James 3:1.

Apollos' example: Acts 18:24-28

Vs.24 He was both eloquent and mighty in the scriptures.
Vs.25 He was teachable, he had a fervent spirit.
Vs.26 He spoke boldly.
Vs.27 He was a great help to the brethren.
Vs.28 He powerfully demonstrated by the scriptures, that Jesus was the Christ.

Teachers have the ability to carefully teach sound doctrine because God has opened their minds and has revealed His word to them. They know how to hear Him and God gives them wisdom to communicate His truth to the people.

The characteristics that the Lord gave through the prophet Isaiah concerning teachers are:

- The Lord GOD hath given me the tongue of the learned; they know how to speak a word to the weary Isaiah 50:4.

- They listen like the learned, the Lord opened their ears and they did not rebel against the heavenly mandate or turn back Isaiah 50:5.

In Ephesians 4:21-24 the apostle Paul tells us what effect the teachings of Christ should bring about in the lives of believers.

Lay aside the old self, which is being corrupted in accordance with the lusts of deceit ... be renewed in the spirit of your mind, and put on the new self, which in the likeness of God ... created in righteousness and holiness of the truth.

CONCLUSION

The five ministries develop, as the vision is carried out and fulfilled.

- The evangelist wins souls (All believers should know how to win souls).
- The pastor is the one who consolidates (Encounters).
- The teacher is the one who teaches (School of Leaders).

- The prophet sets the direction for the disciples.
- The apostle opens the way for the new generations.

EVALUATION

In the final exam it is important for the students to establish the differences and relationships between the gifts of the Spirit, the fruit of the Spirit and the ministry gifts.

RECOMMENDED METHODOLOGY

Open up this class with a brief overview of the history of Christianity. Peak the class' interest by showing examples of men who have impacted entire nations with their ministries. During the discussion invite the students to share examples that they have knowledge of in this area. Then move from this discussion right into teaching on the five ministries.

APPLICATION

Ask each student to identify what their calling is in God's work, according to the ministry gifts given to them by the Holy Spirit.

STUDENTS' ASSIGNMENT

Interview some people in church that are actively functioning in a ministry and ask them how God is using them and what spiritual gifts they have seen operating in their lives.

5 Questionnaire for Further Study

1. What is a ministerial gift? _____
_____
_____
_____
_____

2. What ministerial gift have you been called to? _____
_____
_____
_____
_____

3. What are the characteristics of an Apostle? _____
_____
_____
_____
_____

4. What are the characteristics of a Teacher? _____
_____
_____
_____
_____

5. What are the characteristics of a Prophet? _____
_____
_____
_____
_____

6. What are the characteristics of an Evangelist? _____
_____
_____
_____

7. What are the characteristics of a Pastor? _____

_____

_____

_____

8. Why are the ministerial gifts important within the church?

_____

_____

_____

_____

9. What responsibility do we have towards the calling to ministry? _____

_____

_____

_____

The Importance of Counseling

6
LESSON

TEACHING OBJECTIVE

The goal is that the students learn what counseling in the ministry is and its importance.

STUDENT OBJECTIVE

1   Define counseling.

2   Explain the importance of counseling.

3   Give a biblical example of counseling.

BIBLICAL FOUNDATIONAL
REFERENCE

Exodus 18:13-26

CORRESPONDING
BIBLICAL
FOUNDATION

Exodus 18:13-26

Isaiah 50:4

Ezekiel 3:20-21

2 Corinthians 1:3-4

1 Thessalonians 2:7

James 5:18

John 3:1-15

John 4

Please note that the counseling information on these pages does in no case take away from or make light of those that are in the actual profession of counseling. Be reminded that, as stated on page 61 that the counsel we offer is biblical counseling. Do not be misconstrued by the counseling of licensed professionals outside of our Christian lifestyle.

A. DEFINITION

The word used in the New Testament for counsel is NOUTHESIA, which means to give scriptural direction. In the Old Testament it means to give counsel or direction.

To counsel biblically, the counselor needs to know the scriptures well, have the ability to identify problems and know the right techniques to achieve the desired outcomes.

The purpose of counseling is to cause a change in behavior, emotions and character.

Counseling is a vital component when it is done by the, successful care of disciples. Through it, the leaders will get to know each person well and offer them help and minister to them in the various areas of their lives.

B. IMPORTANCE

Without a doubt, one of the best lessons learned from counseling was the one Moses received from his father-in-law while visiting. He observed that Moses was wearing himself out by trying to do everything himself. He counseled Moses based on his own experience in ministry being that, as he was a priest in Midian.

Exodus 18:13-26

a. Listen to me and I will give you counsel.
b. Stand for the people before God and submit yourself to the things of God.
c. Teach them the laws and how they should walk.

He should delegate responsibilities and choose leaders with the following characteristics:
· Able men.
· Who fear God.
· Men of truth.
· Who hate dishonest gain.

These are the qualifications, spelled out by Moses' father-in-law that make up the leaders of thousands, hundreds, fifties and of tens. With these qualities they would judge the people at all times in small matters while all difficult disputes would be brought to Moses.

And Moses listened to his father-in-law and did all he said.
As they were about to enter the promised land of Canaan, Moses reminded them of the events that had occurred
(Deuteronomy 1:12-17) to prove that he did exactly that.

A counselor should be one who:

- Instructs with his tongue (Isaiah 50:4).
- Helps the righteous ones who fall (Ezekiel 3:20-21).
- Shares his experiences (2 Corinthians 1:3-4).
- Is tender like a nursing mother (1 Thessalonians 2:7).
- Restores the one who has left (James 5:19-20).
- Has a gift to pastor and take care of the flock.
- Is good at detecting problems and ministering to specific needs.
- Helps to develop the character of Christ in others.
- Offers support and fellowship to believers.
- Improves the process of restoration.
- Corrects wrong doctrines.

C. COUNSELING SITUATIONS IN THE BIBLE

Jesus with Nicodemus John 3:1-15
Jesus and the Samaritan woman John 4

CONCLUSION

Counseling is a biblical practice of great importance in the exercise of leadership.
Dr. Tim Denton, a noted Christian counselor suggests this: "God loves us and calls us all to serve Him and to serve one another. Whether you are encouraging a child or caring for an elderly man in deep depression, helping individuals see beyond their pain and circumstances, with the message that God cares about people and will deliver us is the heart of a caring ministry."

EVALUATION

Through a quiz you can check the indicators mentioned above.

RECOMMENDED METHODOLOGY

In the class session combine lecture with question and answer format to develop the subject matter in this lesson.

APPLICATION

Use the people you are winning to Christ, whether it's your family, friends or co-workers to implement the principles you have learned. Keep in mind that you are an instrument through which the Holy Spirit can work.

STUDENTS' ASSIGNMENT

The students should pick one of the biblical examples of counseling and study it and make a presentation explaining the importance of the counsel in that passage.

6 Questionnaire for Further Study

1. What is counseling? _____
_____
_____

2. Why is counseling important within the church? _____
_____
_____

3. Analyze the advice Jethro gave to Moses according to
Exodus 18:13-26: _____
_____
_____

4. Analyze the following counsel and respond:

Jesus with Nicodemus John 3:1-15
Jesus and the Samaritan woman John 4

a. What was their problem? _____
_____
_____

b. How did the Holy Spirit guide Jesus in counseling or advising
them?_____
_____
_____

c. What gifts did Jesus need to discern their problems? _____
_____
_____

d. What was the solution proposed by Jesus? _____
_____
_____

The Application of Counseling

TEACHING OBJECTIVE

The goal is for the student to understand both, who is involved in counseling and their relationships with one another.

STUDENT OBJECTIVE

1 Explain the role of the Holy Spirit in the process of counseling.

2 Explain the role of the counselor in the process of counseling.

3 Explain the role of the person receiving counsel in the process of counseling.

BIBLICAL FOUNDATIONAL
REFERENCE

John 14:26

CORRESPONDING
BIBLICAL
FOUNDATION

John 16:13

John 16:7-8

Luke 12:12

1 Corinthians 2:13

1 John 2:27

Isaiah 11:2

Colossians 3:16

Proverbs 2:6-7

Luke 21:15

James 1:5

PEOPLE INVOLVED IN COUNSELING

The biblical context of counseling always calls for a minimum of three people:

The counselor.
The person counseled.
The Holy Spirit.

A. THE HOLY SPIRIT

One of the names of [the] Holy Spirit is COMFORTER, which comes from the word PARAKLETOS. It is actually synonymous with intercessor or counselor. Given this, we can say that, failing to include Him in counseling and not depending on Him, is an act of self-sufficiency.

We should keep in mind that the works of the Holy Spirit relate to counseling:

- John 14:26	He would teach us and remind us of all things.
- John 16:13	He guides us to all truth.
- John 16:7-8	Convicts us of sin.
- Luke 12:12	Teaches us what to say.
- 1 Corinthians 2:13	We speak with the gifts of the Spirit.
- 1 John 2:27	The anointing teaches us.

B. THE COUNSELOR

Biblical counseling is a job that requires preparation and wisdom. The leader should prepare for this role and be in communication with his leaders so that he is always being supervised in this area.

Requirements for the counselor:

- Extensive knowledge of the Bible
  (Isaiah 11:2 and Colossians 3:16).
- He should be convinced that the Word is true.
  Grounded in it he will motivate and build the faith of
  others. This is important because it helps us to
  know the will of God in each case and keeps us in
  sound doctrine.
- Divine Wisdom.
  (Proverbs 2:6-7, Luke 21:15 and James 1:5).
  It comes from God and is useful to applying
  knowledge in the best possible way, to resolve
  conflicts and find solutions. Wisdom is a gift of God
  (1 Corinthians 12:8); it increases with experience
  (Job 32:7) and we acquire it from prayer and from
  studying the Bible.
- Good will towards others.
- Have LOVE as the foundation of our relationships
  with the brethren in the church. We need to
  seek out what benefits them, showing an
  active interest in trying to help them. Serve others
  being interested in what they need.

The Lord can cause that love to grow (1 Thessalonians 3:12).
It should be a sincere love (Romans 12:9).
Love your neighbor (Matthew 22:39).

Characteristics of a counselor:

- Be emotionally sound
  (Matthew 5:8 and Proverbs 4:23).
- Have general knowledge of human nature.
- Have willingness to listen (James 1:19).
- Be intellectually prepared (read books on the
  subject).
- Be available and committed to the person being
  counseled.
- Have discernment to find solutions to the problems
  through the Bible.
- Be prayerful, seeking divine direction.
- Believe that the person being counseled can change.

C. THE PERSON BEING COUNSELED

We should acknowledge that people are simply different from one another. They each have their way of seeing and living life. They vary in the areas of their cultural, spiritual, social, economic and educational backgrounds. Therefore, it is necessary to get to know them before offering some useful help for their problem.

You need to believe they can change and you must listen and motivate them to do so.

What does the person receiving counsel expect?

- To find a solution to their problem.
- For someone to go to the root of the problem.
- To get help in a time of crisis.
- To help change unwanted behavior.
- To be taught the right things.
- To develop growth and maturity.

CONCLUSION

It is important for counseling to be a dynamic process. It is necessary to be sensitive to the roles played by every person involved.

EVALUATION

The concepts can be evaluated using a quiz or short test.

RECOMMENDED METHODOLOGY

The lecture approach is recommended for this lesson.

STUDENTS' ASSIGNMENT

Complete a project about the role of the Holy Spirit.

7 Questionnaire for Further Study

1. Who are the people involved in counseling? _____
_____
_____

2. What does the Holy Spirit have to do with counseling? _____
_____
_____

3. Draw a line connecting the corresponding verses to the proper text:

John 14:26	He would teach us and remind us of all things.
John 16:13	He guides us to all truth.
John 16:7-8	He convicts us of sin.
Luke 12:12	He teaches us what to say.
1 Corinthians 2:13	We speak with the gifts of the Spirit.
1 John 2:27	The anointing teaches us.

4. Who is the counselor? _____
_____

5. What requirements does a counselor need? _____
_____
_____

6. What are the characteristics of a counselor? _____
_____
_____
_____

7. What does the counseled person expect? _____
_____

8. Who is the counseled person? _____

9. What attitude should the person being counseled have?
_____

The Practice of Biblical Counseling

TEACHER OBJECTIVE

The goal is for the students to understand the key points to keep in mind during counseling.

STUDENT OBJECTIVE

1 Explain the suggestions to perform counseling.

2 Explain the recommendations given for the process of counseling.

THE PRACTICE OF BIBLICAL COUNSELING

A. SUGGESTIONS FOR COUNSELING

Some cases will require only one session. Others will require several planned sessions, depending on the problem.

- Start and end the session with a word of prayer.
- Listen attentively to the person when talking about problem.
- Ask questions that relate to the problem.
- Offer solutions for each area of concern.
- Set clear goals for what needs to be accomplished.
- Support each solution with a biblical foundation.
- Evaluate progress (if it requires several sessions).
- Assign tasks that reinforce the goals.
- Write letters.
- Use projects that require action.
- If possible, involve the people that are related to the problem.
- Involve the leader also and make him part of the solution.
- Be prepared for the time of ministry.
- Have recommended reading. Offer it as a part of the healing process.

B. RECOMMENDATIONS

Good counseling can be summed up when you know these things:

1. What is the specific problem(s)? (You should understand the problem in detail).

2. What biblical principles apply? What does the bible say about

this issue? (It is good for them to be the ones looking up the verses and explaining what they understand).

3. How to apply the biblical principles to solve this case?

4. Listen attentively to what is being spoken and how. If for example harsh expressions, are used that the person may not be aware of, that can be a way of helping them to discover what the problem may be. Sometimes the problem is unknown, a word of wisdom or of knowledge is needed to discern it. You will also notice that frustrations, hidden feelings, fixations and excuses have produced habits that have generated problems.

5. The counselor should repeat or summarize in his own words what the person has said. This serves to verify if the communication is good and will avoid misunderstandings and ambiguities.

6. The counselor should remember that communication is not only verbal but also physical. Close attention should be paid to the body language such as, facial expressions, gestures, body posture and tone of voice.

7. Show respect, acceptance and trust for the person so that they feel free to express their feelings and thoughts. The counselor should lay aside any type of prejudice.

8. It is important to identify the feelings that they have toward the problem and towards the people that are involved in the problem and then it needs to be confronted with the Word of God.

C. COMMON CASES

- Personal conflicts.
- Interpersonal relationships.
- Past memories.
- Financial problems.
- Spiritual and doctrinal problems.
- Sin.
- Relationship with God.
- Family problems (i.e., spouse, marriage).

CONCLUSION

You need to be sensitive and acquire wisdom in order for the counseling to be performed correctly.

EVALUATION

In the test for this lesson, you should propose a case for the students to try to solve using the concepts learned in class.

RECOMMENDED METHODOLOGY

The lecture method can be used but because it is a vast subject, other resources are recommended as supplements such as note cards, handouts, posters, etc.

STUDENTS' ASSIGNMENT

Surely your students have already had the experience of counseling someone. Have them describe a case they have had and how they counseled using the things taught in class.

8 Questionnaire for Further Study

1. Explain the steps needed for excellent biblical counseling:

   _____
   _____
   _____
   _____
   _____

2. What are the necessary recommendations for good counseling? _____
   _____
   _____
   _____

3. Find verses for the following cases:

   a. Rejection
   b. Divorce
   c. Sin
   d. Family problems
   e. Resentment
   f. Past memories

4. How do you apply the biblical principles to each case? _____
   _____
   _____
   _____
   _____
   _____

5. Prepare a chart for reference and support in each case:

PROBLEM   BIBLE VERSES   POSSIBLE SOLUTIONS

Key Themes in Counseling

LESSON

TEACHING OBJECTIVE

The goal for the student is to become better able to handle the proper bible verses pertaining to specific problems.

STUDENT OBJECTIVE

1   To know the bible verses for specific problems.

2   Relating specific problems with proper bible verses.

DEVELOPMENT OF THE SUBJECT

According to the following topics, the student should look up bible verses that correspond with the subject that show God's point of view. It will offer solutions. They will share them with the class.

ARGUMENTS

Proverbs 15:1-9   The mouth of the wise.
Proverbs 26:17-28   The lips of the fool.
Philippians 2:12-18   Correct behavior.
Titus 3:1-11   The power of regeneration.

ATTITUDE

Philippians 2:5-8   Behave like Jesus did.
Philippians 4:4-9   To guard our emotions, mind and will.

DEPRESSION

1 Kings 19:1-9   Elijah's depression.
Psalm 42:1-11   A battle of faith in God.
Psalm 40:1-3   Coming out of depression.

FEAR

Joshua 1:1-9	Effort and courage are the antidote to discouragement.
Psalm 27:1	God gives us strength to overcome fear.
Psalm 91:1-16	A good relationship with God brings protection from dangers and sudden calamities or disasters.
Psalm 121:1-8	Have confidence that our help and refuge is in the Lord.
Proverbs 29:25	Trusting in the Lord bring Safety.

FRUSTRATION

Job 6:11-15	Job felt let down by his friends and by God.
Job 7:1-21	Job describes all the adversity he has lived through but ends in asking God to take away his rebellion and to forgive his sins.
Ephesians 6:10-18	With the armor of God on, you can break frustration.

JOY

Matthew 5:1-12	The Lord shows us what will bring joy to our hearts.
Matthew 25:21	Jesus rewards the faithful with eternal joy.
Luke 15:6-10	There is joy in heaven for the repented sinner.
1 Peter 1:8-9	Faith produces unspeakable joy.
Hebrews 1:9	Jesus was anointed with the oil of gladness.
1 Peter 4:13	The joy that there is in suffering.
James 1:2-6	The spiritual power to withstand adversity.

INFERIORITY

| 1 Samuel 15:17 | Feeling small in your own eyes. Because of this, he (Saul) gave room to fear and lost his relationship with God. |
| Numbers 13:33 | Feeling insignificant in front of others. This caused the Israelites to begin complaining |

and as a result, they lost their faith and had to wander in the wilderness for forty years.

2 Samuel 7:8	Believing that you cause repulsion in others. Saul's grandson has an inferiority complex and began believing that his life was a mistake.
Psalm 139:13-16	We should remember that we were created by the power of God.
1 Cor 1:26-29	God did not choose us because of our appearance or abilities or wisdom but because of his pure mercy.
1 Peter 2:9-10	We are a chosen generation, a royal priest hood, a people purchased by God.

MORALITY

Job 31:1	Helps us to avoid the demands of lust.
Matthew 19:16-26	There is no salvation in morality.
Luke 17:26-30	The moral decline of the people would be like in the days of Noah.
Roman 2:14-15	You should have a clear conscience.
1 Corinthians 15:3	Do not partake of evil conversations.
2 Corinthians 5:17	We are new creatures as a result of the new birth.

RESENTMENT

1 Samuel 26:1-11	David left all resentment in God's hands.
Isaiah 45:9-10	Some resent God and their parents too.
Luke 15:11-32	The brother of the prodigal son resented that the banquet was not been for him.

SEX

Genesis 4:1-2, 25	A God given method for having children.
Genesis 18:12	Sex brings delight.
Genesis 39:6-7	Some men are attractive to certain wome but this is a dangerous game.
Ephesians 5:25,26	Love and sexuality
Proverbs 5:15-21	An exclusive privilege for marriage. Extra marital relationships should not be permited.
Proverbs 6:23-26	The Word is able to keep us from the deceit of the strange woman.
Song of Solomon 5:4	An attraction that moves our heart.
Ezekiel 16:8	There is a time for love.
1 Corinthians 7:5	Abstinence in marriage should be for prayer.
Hebrews 13:4	The sanctity of the marriage bed.
1 Thessalonians 4:1-8	It is important to know what type of life pleases God.

CONCLUSION

It is important for the leadership to provide solutions to the problems of the disciples according to biblical principles.

RECOMMENDED METHODOLOGY

The professor should write on the board a specific problem and ask the students to look for the correct biblical foundation to purpose proper counsel. Guide the class as the problems are worked out and teach them about the solutions.

STUDENTS' ASSIGNMENT

Study each of the texts provided and find some for other problems that may also be considered important. Prepare for the workshop in the next class.

9 Questionnaire for Further Study

1. What is an argument? _____
_____
_____
_____

2. What are the most frequent arguments? _____
_____
_____
_____
_____

3. Find at least three problems and from God's point of view, offer solutions. _____
_____
_____
_____
_____

4. Has biblical counseling helped you? How were you able to overcome your problems? _____
_____
_____
_____
_____

Counseling Workshop

TEACHING OBJECTIVE

The goal is for the student to develop the ability to find possible solutions to a given case.

STUDENT OBJECTIVE

1 Give solutions to a specific case according to the recommendations given and with the biblical references cited.

2 Relate the concepts of the previous lessons to a specific case.

The professor should find cases that call for counseling. Have them written out and revised, hand them out to the class by groups. Once all the cases are assigned, the students will:

1) Find bible references.
2) Create questions that generate more information.
3) Offer possible solutions.
4) Assign tasks and determine how to minister.

You need to keep in mind everything taught in the seminar. The work that went into developing these cases can be enhanced by reading informative books on the subject of counseling. It would also be good to speak with those who are experienced in counseling.

Have the students hand in their written homework to you and guide each group along as they are completing their activity.

1. I have not consecrated myself because of all the pressures at home...
2. I don't understand why I have to leave my worldly friends...
3. I don't feel comfortable in any group...
4. I still don't really feel forgiven by God...

EVALUATION

Take definite notice of how the students involve themselves in this project. From your observation, assess their understanding of this lesson. Their involvement will also tell a lot about the instructor's teaching. However, on the test, include the most important aspects of this lesson for the students to answer.

10 Questionnaire for Further Study

1. Practice with three or four people and evaluate the following:

a. The counselor
b. The problem

- Bible references
- God's point of view
- The solution

c. The person being counseled

2. Have a time of prayer and thank God for what you learned in this seminar and ask for wisdom to be an excellent counselor.